Markus Moser

Implementierung einer GUI-Applikation zur optimalen Zuordnung von Studenten mittels Java/Swing

GRIN Verlag

Bibliografische Information der Deutschen Nationalbibliothek:

Die Deutsche Bibliothek verzeichnet diese Publikation in der Deutschen National-
bibliografie; detaillierte bibliografische Daten sind im Internet über http://dnb.d-
nb.de/ abrufbar.

Imprint:

Copyright © 2008 GRIN Verlag GmbH
Druck und Bindung: Books on Demand GmbH, Norderstedt Germany
ISBN: 978-3-640-83677-2

This book at GRIN:

http://www.grin.com/en/e-book/166912/implementierung-einer-gui-applikation-
zur-optimalen-zuordnung-von-studenten

GRIN - Your knowledge has value

Der GRIN Verlag publiziert seit 1998 wissenschaftliche Arbeiten von Studenten, Hochschullehrern und anderen Akademikern als eBook und gedrucktes Buch. Die Verlagswebsite www.grin.com ist die ideale Plattform zur Veröffentlichung von Hausarbeiten, Abschlussarbeiten, wissenschaftlichen Aufsätzen, Dissertationen und Fachbüchern.

Visit us on the internet:

http://www.grin.com/

http://www.facebook.com/grincom

http://www.twitter.com/grin_com

WIRTSCHAFTSUNIVERSITÄT WIEN
BAKKALAUREATSARBEIT

Titel der Bakkalaureatsarbeit:
"JAssign" - Implementierung einer GUI-Applikation zur optimalen Zuordnung von Studenten mittels Java/Swing

Englischer Titel der Bakkalaureatsarbeit:
"JAssign" - Implementation of a GUI-application for the optimal assignment of students employing Java/Swing

VerfasserIn: Markus Moser

Studienrichtung: Wirtschaftsinformatik
Kurs: 996 IT-Praktikum mit Bakkalaureatsarbeit
Textsprache   Englisch

Deutsche Zusammenfassung

Schlüsselworte

Java, Swing, GUI, lineare Optimierung, Studentenzuteilung

JAssign ist eine auf *Java* basierende Anwendung zur Zuteilung von Studenten zu Projekten innerhalb einer Lehrveranstaltung unter Berücksichtigung ihrer individuellen Präferenzen die zur Reihung der Projekte verwendet werden. Die Interaktion mit dem Programm erfolgt über eine graphische Benutzeroberfläche (graphical user interface) welche auf *Swing* basiert und das Importieren, Exportieren oder Verändern der Daten oder Festlegen von Einstellungen für den Optimierungsprozess ermöglicht. Diese Bakkalaureatsarbeit dokumentiert die Architektur und Funktionalität der Anwendung. Ebenso ist eine grundlegende Beschreibung des *Java Swing* Toolkits enthalten.

English abstract

Key Words

Java, Swing, GUI, linear optimization, student allocation

JAssign is a *Java*-based application to assign students to topics of a university course according to their individual preferences used for ranking these topics. Interaction with the program can be conducted over a graphical user interface based on *Swing* which allows importing, exporting or modifying the data and setting constraints for the optimization process. This bachelor thesis documents the architecture and main functionality of the application. It also provides a basic description of *Java's Swing* toolkit.

Contents

List of Figures

1 Project description of JAssign

1.1 Introduction

In some university courses several topics exist for the participants to choose from. Almost certainly, if the number of topics is smaller than the number of participating students, problems about matching each student with a topic will arise. If students are given the possibility to rank the available topics freely by assigning numerical preferences and working in groups is also permitted or even mandatory, the process of assigning is prone to lead to a clash of interests. The possibility of randomly assigning the participants is likely to yield even less satisfactory results and will ignore the individual preferences. Additionally, if upper and lower boundaries for the number of students in each group exist, the question of allocation becomes even more complex. The process of group-building and assigning the participants to different projects with an emphasis on their preference can be done manually with the help of pen and paper, which is a tedious and time-consuming task and makes the use of an application to solve this problem reasonable. Strictly mathematically speaking this is a problem of linear optimization which can be solved efficiently following known algorithms. The aim of this project is the development of a *Java* application with a graphical user interface, based on the *Swing* toolkit distributed with *Java*, that provides the functionality to assign students to groups according to their preferences.

An implementation of a similar application with a similar functional scope already exists, the main differences arise from the choice of platform and technology. The predecessor is a *Java-EE* (Java Enterprise Edition) application which was developed for a web context and employs technologies especially created for the purpose of fostering web-based, location-independent applications. The system operates on a client-server architecture and uses a role-based access model which incorporates individual views for students, lecturers and admins, including extensive help. To provide efficient data handling a relational DBMS is used. This system is fully documented and will be an available reference throughout the development of JAssign. A spreadsheet-based version written in Excel additionally exists which also deals with the specified allocation problem.

1.2 System specifications

Basic functionality

- Stand-alone architecture that does not require network access.

- Usage of technological framework of *Java* and the *JDK*.

- Runs inside a *Java Runtime Environment* which makes the application basically platform independent, a feature that is one of the hallmarks of *Java*.

- Graphical components employ and follow the standards of the *Java Swing Framework*, a collection of classes especially designed for the creation of graphical user interfaces. Regarding alignment and design of the widgets, the GUI shall be easy to use and intuitive in terms of usability.

- Provides the necessary functions to allow users to import or export data used for the internal assignment process in a widespread and commonly used plaintext format. Importing and exporting to CSV (Comma separated values) is supported.

- The results of the optimization process are displayed in a formatted and presentable view that is suited for printing. To accomplish this, a feature that allows exporting to a newly created PDF file is implemented.

- The user's interaction with the application is conducted over a graphical user interface (GUI) which provides commonly used widgets and visual elements that conceal the complexity of the real application and offer the user convenient means to interact with the program.

- The language used throughout the application and auxiliary documentation will be English.

- An extensive help feature which mainly uses tooltips facilitates user interaction.

- External libraries are used to provide highly complex functions which would be extremely intricate to develop. These libraries are included and harnessed under the terms and conditions of their licenses.

  - The library `lp_solve`, which is publicly available under the *LGPL* (Lesser GNU Public License) is used for problems pertaining to linear optimization.

  - The *Java* library *iText* offers convenient methods to create and write a pdf document from within *Java* and is used for exporting the formatted results to PDF.

- Architecture and design of the application are implemented on a modular basis to allow further extension.

Use-Cases

This section describes the logical and functional interactions from the user perspective. As this is a standalone-application, the creation of different roles and perspectives is not required. The user's perspective is generally expected to be the role of the lecturer whose main concern is the assignment of the participants to the tendered topics. Figure 1.1 shows a use-case diagram. The user can:

- specify an external file (csv) as source of the data to be imported. Additionally the number of lines to be skipped and the separation character which denotes the position of an entry inside the csv-file can be defined.

- modify the imported or inserted data in a convenient way.

- create and modify the projects (topics) that are available for distribution.

- specify the minimal and maximal number of participants for each project in advance.

- alter the given preferences and modify the results of the optimization process by changing the assignment.

- specify categories which serve as constraints and ensure a projects is or is not assigned to particular students.

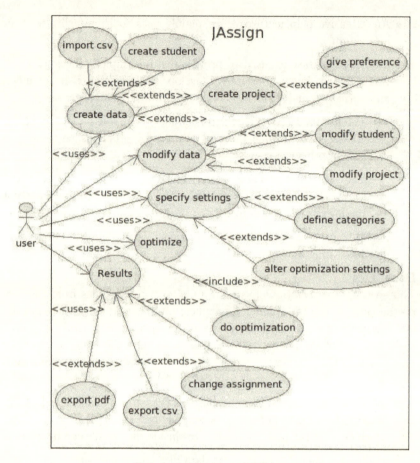

Figure 1.1: Use-cases of JAssign

- influence the optimization process in advance by specifying constraints and parameters for each student and project.

1.3 Available legacy systems and resources

OptAssign is a *Java-EE* based application for assigning students to topics within university courses (Waglechner, 2008). Its core functionality shall be sketched to briefly show its features and outline the functional connection to JAssign. *OptAssign* employs a MySQL-based database which is integrated with the help of the *Java Persistence API*. The external library `lp_solve` provides a wrapper for *Java* and is used for solving the problem of optimization which is done by translating it into a linear model. Using a server-client architecture, *OptAssign* provides a web-based interface for access, which is based on a role model that allows several types of users with different permissions to perform the actions typical for their role. Three types of roles are intended: **Administrator** for general administration of the assembled data and registered users, **Course Lecturer** to create and delete courses, admit students and execute the optimization process in order to assign these students to a particular course. A user of the role **Student** can rank the projects available for distribution by assigning individual preferences to them.

The core optimization model takes each student's preferences into account upon calculating the optimal assignment of these students to the tendered projects.

OptAssign shares the core of the optimization feature and some of the use-cases with JAssign.

The core of the optimization feature of *OptAssign* will be adapted to suit the data and technology of JAssign and thus serve as a reference, everything else will have to be developed from ground-up. An in-depth description of the mathematical optimization model is included in the Appendix.

1.4 Project schedule

Project aims

- Development of a standalone application optimally assigning students to projects in university courses.

- Testing the application in a productive environment and ensure it runs inside the JRE on Windows and Linux.

- Writing a complete documentation.

Non-aims

- Extending the web-based application.

- Add other languages apart from English or provide an architecture for multilingual extensions.

- Checking data for corruption or logical faults on import.

- Data maintenance or data collection.

- Extending and maintaining the final application after completion of the functional product.

1.5 Project Milestones

PSP-ID	Milestone	Basic dates	Planned dates	Acutal dates
4	Project started	13.3.2008	13.3.2008	13.3.2008
18	Design completed	25.3.2008	25.3.2008	31.3.2008
23	Program implemented	1.5.2008	1.5.2008	14.5.2008
36	Program ready for productive use	20.5.2008	20.5.2008	9.6.2008
8	Project completed	20.6.2008	20.6.2008	20.6.2008

Table 1.1: Project Milestones

1.6 Structured plan

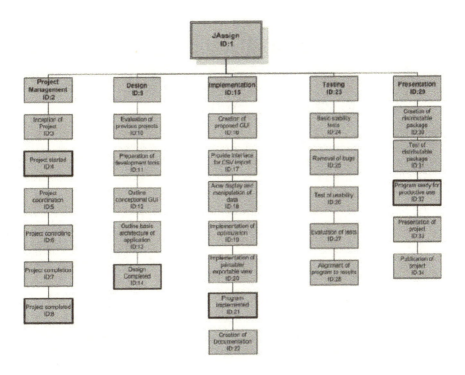

Figure 1.2: Structured plan

2 Creation of a GUI with Java / Swing

2.1 Basic description of Swing

Specially designed for the purpose of creating graphical user interfaces, the *Java Foundation Classes* were conceived to provide a framework and offer abundant features for interactivity and graphical display. The JFC classes consist of several different components that are closely intertwined to provide the functionality of a fully-fledged GUI. The following section will focus only on the *Swing* GUI components which are vital building blocks of every *Java*-based graphical application. *Swing* is the successor of *Java's Abstract Window Toolkit*, an earlier implementation of user interface components, however, it still makes use of *AWT* components to some extent.

Additionally, a framework for creating applications exists. The *Swing Application Framework* is a set of *Java* classes helping to design applications by providing designs that are common to typical applications and can be reused. "The Swing Application Framework is a light framework that simplifies the creation and maintaining of small- to medium-sized *Java* desktop applications" (Sun Microsystems, 2008d). *Java* Specification Request 296 defines it as "...will provide a simple application framework for Swing applications. It will define infrastructure common to most desktop applications. In so doing, Swing applications will be easier to create" (Sun Microsystems, 2006).

The *Swing* classes provide elements that can be arranged and aligned in a desired order to serve as a graphical user interface. These components are predefined to a certain extent and can be regarded as general templates, yet they are highly customizable. Most components include predefined features such as sorting or drag and drop. The functionality of *Swing* is not limited to providing a collection of widgets, as a complete toolkit it also includes features such as event handling and window management. *Swing* components

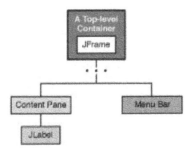

Figure 2.1: Component hierarchy of Swing, Source: (Sun Microsystems, 2008a)

were designed to work the same on all platforms, to the maximum degree possible (Sun Microsystems, 2008c). Some of the more important components which have been used for the development of this application shall be described in the following sections.

The design of Swing components needs to adhere strictly to a predefined *containment hierarchy*, which can be regarded as a tree of all components displaying onscreen. A top-level container serves as provider of a content pane, which then contains the visible, non-menu elements. In a standalone *Java*-application this role is usually assumed by a JFrame, in applets a JApplet component can serve as root. Additionally, a menu bar can be inserted into the top-level frame to include the functionality of a typical menu. Each program that uses *Swing* components has at least one top-level container and a component hierarchy, but also multiple are possible if more than one top-level container is implemented (Sun Microsystems, 2008a).

Figure 2.1 shows the component hierarchy of a typical application:

Elements can be directly added to the content pane, an example to accomplish this is the following method:
```
frame.getContentPane().add(mybutton, BorderLayout.CENTER);
```

Here the second parameter specifies the layout manager to be used, defining the way in which the added components are to be aligned. Several layouts exist and *Java* tries to evaluate the position of the element preceding this parameter. However, the clear alignment of the different elements is not easily achieved, so the layout parameters have to be handled carefully.

Top-level containers should not be confused with the root pane, another intermediate container which manages the content pane and the menu bar. The presence of root panes is usually negligible for the typical developer, it can, however, be useful if intercepting mouse clicks or actions extending over multiple components is desired (Sun Microsystems, 2008a).

NetBeans IDE   The integrated development environment *NetBeans* IDE has several features which greatly facilitate the creation of a GUI or any *Java* application. *NetBeans* includes several *GUI Tools* for the creation of sophisticated GUIs. Especially the *GUI Builder* (code named project *Matisse*), which was introduced in version 5.0 of the IDE, was designed to assist the developer in designing and building *Java* forms (Sun Microsystems, 2008b). Aligning the components of a GUI manually is challenging and prone to errors as the outcome can only be seen upon compiling, the *GUI Builder* of *NetBeans* does not only show a realistic preview but also allows editing and placing these components by drag and drop. This also applies to the positioning of the elements, thus ensuring the user's alignment is maintained. "The GUI Builder enables you to lay out forms by placing components where you want them and by providing visual feedback in the form of guidelines" (Sun Microsystems, 2008d). Its automatic code generation feature embeds the GUI into *Java* code, concealing the complexity of the components' generation and arrangement, which allows the developer to focus on the application logic. The code generated by the *GUI Builder* is highlighted as *Guarded Block*, making it not directly editable.

The Swing Application Framework

NetBeans is designed to fully support the *Swing Application Framework*, which can serve as a template for building *Swing*-based applications. "The framework's primary goal is to provide the kernel of a typical Swing application, helping programmers to get started quickly and to adopt best practices for just a few elements common to every Swing application: architecture, lifecycle, resource management, event handling, threading, session state, and local storage" (O'Conner, 2007). Basically, two classes exist to help managing an application: `Application` and `ApplicationContext`, with a 1:1 relationship between them. `ApplicationContext` provides services to the application. Programs using the *Swing Application Framework* must extend the `Application` class or its `SingleFrameApplication` subclass. `Application` provides lifecycle methods for launching the application, initializing the user interface and shutting down. `SingleFrameApplication` adds a default main GUI frame, retrieves and injects default resources, and uses the Application-Context to save and restore simple session state (O'Conner, 2007). The framework also handles resources such as icons, font definitions and text and supports multiple locales which makes translations to other languages easy. Resources are stored for each class in a file with a `.properties` suffix.

2.2 Commonly used widgets

In the *Swing* class hierarchy the name of many components starts with the letter J, which indicates that they descend from the `JComponent` class. That implies that all widgets, like `JButton`, `JTable`, `JTextField` inherit methods from their superclass `JComponent`, which extends the `Container` class, which itself extends the class `Component`. A variety of features is provided by the Component class: "The Component class includes everything from providing layout hints to supporting painting and events. The Container class has support for adding components to the container and laying them out" (Sun Microsystems, 2008a).

JComponent also provides a large variety of features such as:

- Tool tips: The simplest but must effective way of providing help to the user about a component. When the mouse pointer hovers over a component for a brief period of time, a small popup text appears near the component.

- Painting and borders: Allows specifying how the borders of a component are drawn. Prespecified methods can be overridden to perform custom painting inside components.

- Custom properties: One or more properties can be associated with any `JComponent`.

- Support for layout: Allows setting the layout and completes the layout methods of `Component` by providing setter methods.

(Sun Microsystems, 2008c)

Any element that inherits from JComponent must be placed inside a containment hierarchy with a top-level container as root. These top-level containers (`JFrame`, `JApplet`, `JDialog`) are specialized classes that are designed to provide a place for other components to draw themselves. Though starting with J, they do not extend `JComponent`.

Some of the more complex components that were used for the development of JAssign are described on the following pages with their most distinctive features in mind, following the descriptions of the API (Sun Microsystems, 2008c).

JTabbedPane

Tabbed panes are perfectly suited for having multiple components share the same space. This is accomplished by providing a clickable label for each contained component, that allows the user to select the active component which is then displayed in full size - a concept known as tabbing, familiar to almost every user of a GUI and one of the most fundamental assets for arranging GUI elements in a spacially efficient way. JTabbedPanes can be used for, but are not limited to containers such as panels. Panels such as JPanel are simple containers for drawing objects.

A tabbed pane in *Java* comes with a broad number of predefined features. New tabs can be added with the `addTab` method, which takes the component to be added as one of its parameters. Tabs are represented by an index corresponding to their position, starting with 0 for the first tab. The title of a tab is not limited to a text, any Component can be specified to serve in this place. A user can simply switch between the different tabs by clicking on

tab with a given title and/or icon. A default JTabbedPane handles the event
listening automatically, so simply adding the component/tabs is sufficient to
build a working implementation of a JTabbedPane.

JTable

JTables are useful widgets for displaying two-dimensional tables of cells,
which can be modified by the user. JTable does not work or provide its
own data, instead it shows a view of the data it is linked to. Each JTable
comprises of different layers which can be regarded separately. A table model
object is used to manage the actual table data. These components (Table,
TableModel, Data) can be regarded as separate. Each table model must
implement the TableModel interface, if none is provided within the program,
JTable automatically creates an instance of DefaultTableModel. A simple
table can be initialized with the following code:

```
TableModel dataModel = new AbstractTableModel() {
public int getColumnCount() { return 10; }
public int getRowCount() { return 10;}
public Object getValueAt(int row, int col)
{ return new Integer(row*col); }
};
JTable table = new JTable(dataModel);
JScrollPane scrollpane = new JScrollPane(table);
```

In this example the table is placed inside a JScrollPane which makes it
scrollable if the amount of data rows exceeds the actual size of the table.
Here the table model is created by instantiating an AbstractTableModel
and providing the abstract methods that need to be specified.
The DefaultTableModel uses a Vector of Vectors or Objects to store cell
values. By using a TableModel interface, the data can also wrapped in the
methods of TableModel and thus passed to JTable directly. If different
types of data are used, this method is more useful as it allows the model to
decide which internal representation to use. The API suggests that as a rule
of thumb, AbstractTableModel is recommendable for creating subclasses

while `DefaultTableModel` is the better choice when subclassing is not required.

There are two constructors that directly accept data:

1. JTable (Object[][] rowData, Object[] columnNames)

2. JTable (Vector rawData, Vector columnnames)

However, these constructors have several drawbacks. The data has to be passed as a vector or array and all values are treated as strings.

`JTable` uses solely integers to refer to the rows and columns of the model it uses. The method `getValueAt(int, int)` can be used to retrieve the contents of a cell (as `Object`).

A `JTable` allows the user to edit the contents of individual cells or make a selection of rows which can be either arbitrary or contiguous. If a single cell is selected it is outlined to show the current focus. If multiple cells are selected the last cell selected by the user is emphasized likewise. Three selection modes for rows exist which can be applied using the `setSelectionMode(int selectionMode)` method. Either single selections, a single contiguous interval, or multiple intervals can be passed as arguments.

A table model can be assigned a set of listeners to deal with changes of the table data. All listeners are instances of `TableModelListener` which itself is a subclass of `EventListener`. Each `TableModelListener` interface used has to specify its implementation of the `tableChanged(TableModelEvent e)` method. `TableModelEvent` notifies listeners about changes within a table model, the exact range of rows, columns or cells that changed can be determined.

Editors and Renderers: For performance reasons, cells are not individual components but treated differently. A *cell renderer* is used to display cells containing the same type of data. "You can think of the renderer as a configurable ink stamp that the table uses to stamp appropriately formatted data onto each cell" (Sun Microsystems, 2008c). Anytime the user starts editing a cell, a *cell editor* takes over the cell that is being edited and controls its behavior. Cell Renderers can be customly specified for each column. If no renderer is specified, the table determines the data type of the column's cells by invoking the `getColumnClass` method. Some data types are predefined, such as *boolean*, *date* or *Icon*. If the data type is `Object`, the object's toString value is displayed inside the cell.

Additionally the cells of a table can also be used for displaying tool tips.

JList

"A component that displays a list of objects and allows the user to select one or more items" (Sun Microsystems, 2008c). The concept of logically separating the view from the content which was introduced in the section on JTable also applies here. A ListModel maintains the content of a list. A table can be instantiated by providing the data as array or Vector of objects, likewise, a list can be created by simply passing the data as argument in its constructor methods. Additionally, a model can by specified by using the setModel method. A DefaultListModel can be used as a convenient solution for creating list models, if desired, an AbstractListModel provides more support for customizing the default methods and listeners.

A JList allows the selection of one or more entries. Three different selection modes can be set with setSelectionMode(int selectionMode). SINGLE_SELECTION (only one entry at a time), SINGLE_INTERVAL_SELECTION (one contiguous interval), MULTIPLE_INTERVAL_SELECTION (no restriction on selecting, this is the default mode). The selection state is managed by an instance of ListSelectionModel.

Event listeners

To provide convenient means of interaction with the application, *Java/Swing* provides a number of listeners that monitor the application's components for change and trigger actions if an interaction is detected. Every event listener has a single argument which is an object that extends the EventObject class. The class EventObject is the common superclass of *AWT* and *Swing* events and contains information about the event. This information may vary, depending on the event, usually describing where the event occurred.

Events can be divided into two groups. Low-level events are events that are triggered directly by user input, such as mouse or key events. Semantic events are more complex and include action and item events. A semantic event might be triggered by the user, there are, however, also semantic events that are not triggered by these low-level interactions. The *Swing* tutorial names as example a table-model event that is fired when the model receives new data from the database. Semantic event listeners have the advantage of being more flexible and robust. For instance, a button will react correctly when it is both clicked or confirmed by pressing return after selection. Some components even require semantic event listeners as they are too complex to register every single event listener that is possibly executed in the context of its look-and-feel (Sun Microsystems, 2008a).

Listeners are interfaces that provide one method or more for the matching events. These interface methods must be implemented when a listener is created. If no implementation of a particular method is desired, the method's body can be left empty. To avoid the problem of maintaining multiple interface methods, *adapter classes* can be implemented which exist for listener interfaces with more than one method.

The problem of implementing multiple listeners that inherit from different classes can be solved by creating so-called `inner classes`. `Inner classes` are class definitions within an existing class, which are permitted by *Java*, as they allow to keep the number of separate classes low. As further extension of this concept, `anonymous inner classes` can be specified which don't need a separate class definition. An example taken from JAssign demonstrates this construct:

```
model.addTableModelListener(new TableModelListener() {
public void tableChanged(TableModelEvent arg0) {
//event-handling code
}});
```

Brief description of commonly used listeners

- *Action listener*: A simple listener that is triggered whenever the user performs an action. This applies to choosing items, clicking buttons or pressing return.

- *Focus listener*: Fires focus events whenever a component gains or looses keyboard focus.

- *Item listener*: Listens for state changes of components having an on/off logic.

- *Table model listener*: Monitors a table for changes. The exact location and range of cells, columns and rows that changed can be determined.

Tooltips in Java

In *Java* any object inheriting from JComponent can display its custom tooltip. Tooltips can be defined as simple pop-up messages that provide a closer description of a visual element if the mouse pointer hovers over the element for a certain duration. They are frequently used for providing quick and accessible help messages. The method setToolTipText(String text) sets the text to be shown as tooltip. Components with multiple parts, such as JTabbedPanes have a setToolTipTextAt(int index, String text) method. Even on components that do not inherit these methods, tooltips can be defined by providing a custom renderer.

As these methods should suffice for creating tooltips, implementing a new instance of JToolTip is not necessary. Additionally, a ToolTipManager exists for each application which allows the specification of tooltip-related parameters like the duration of a tooltip's visibility or the delay of its popup or if the tooltips should be shown at all.

3 Implementation

Although the *Java-EE* application *OptAssign* has served as a role model throughout the implementation of this project and both provide similar optimization features, JAssign was written as a completely separate application using *Java SE* (Standard Edition). Portions of *OptAssign*'s code for building the linear model and performing the optimization were reused for development of the application package, though they had to be largely modified to work without persistent objects and adapted to the data model of classes used in JAssign.

A detailed description of the logical structure of the program and its core features is provided in this section with an in-depth description of each package.

3.1 The class structure of JAssign

The application comprises several top-level packages that logically divide the application into several blocks, each fulfilling a different function. *Java* packages can be regarded as a collection of classes that logically belong together. Structuring a program by grouping classes into packages makes the program significantly more comprehensible and clear.

In JAssign, four different packages can be distinguished.

1. The **main** package, including the main class of the application, which itself contains the definition and alignment of all visual GUI elements together with their listeners and event-handling methods.

2. The **datatype** package contains the basic classes that can be instantiated for creating basic objects such as students and projects. Their basic interconnections make them displayable as a logical data model.

3. The **functions** package provides classes for processing and manipulating internal and external data.

4. The **optimize** package consists of all classes related to linear optimization.

3.2 External libraries used

lpsolve

As mentioned previously, an external library is used to solve problems pertaining to linear programming. The library `lp_solve` provides the necessary functions, which makes it technically an API. `Lp_solve` is "a free (see LGPL for the GNU lesser general public license) linear (integer) programming solver based on the revised simplex method and the Branch-and-bound method for the integers" (M. Berkelaar and Notebaert, 2008). It can solve problems demanding some of the variables to be integers (Mixed integer (MILP or MIP) problems) and is also applicable to problems that only involve integers (ILP or IP problems), as opposed to fractional values.

Though this is not obvious, integer problems are significantly harder to solve in theory and practice. The optimization problem of JAssign arising from the optimal assignment of students to projects is an integer problem. The previously mentioned `Branch-and-bound-method` is based on two basic operations that are applied recursively:

- Branch: The space of all feasible solutions is repeatedly partitioned into smaller and smaller subsets.

- Bound: After each partitioning, those subsets with a bound that exceeds the cost of a known feasible solution are excluded from all further partitionings.

The partition continues until a feasible solution is found (Lawler and Wood, 1966).

In order to be solved, a model needs to be passed to `lp_solve` in matrix representation. Each row of the matrix represents a linear equation and each

column stands for a variable (Waglechner, 2008).
The latest version available at the time of development is `lp_solve 5.5.0.12`
The library itself is written in ANSI C and can be compiled on several platforms, including Windows and Linux. Several wrappers for common programming languages and applications exist which allow an easy integration
of `lp_solve` into *C, Java, .NET* programs or *Microsoft Excel, Matlab* and
several others (M. Berkelaar and Notebaert, 2008).
The API is completely documented, detailed information on all provided
methods can be obtained from `http://lpsolve.sourceforge.net/5.5/`
`lp_solveAPIreference.htm`.

The libraries (or their linux equivalent) of `lp_solve` need to be copied into a
directory accessible as path such as *windows**system32* or */usr/lib* on linux
in order for the optimization to function.

iText

iText is a library developed for *Java* that allows the dynamic generation or
manipulation of PDF files, written by Bruno Lowagie and Paulo Soares. The
portable document format (PDF) has become the most widespread format
for documents, its major benefit is the independence of the document from
the program it is displayed in.
"PDF is the 'Portable Document Format', i.e. the native file format of the
Adobe(®) Acrobat(®) family of products. The goal of these products is to
enable users to exchange and view electronic documents easily and reliably,
independent of the environment in which they were created" (Lowagie, 2008).
iText is not intended as end-user tool and instead designed to be built
into applications to automate the generation of PDF output. The library
provides an extensive and well-documented collection of methods. iText's
API documentation is available at `http://www.1t3xt.info/api/`. iText
is available for free under a multiple license: MPL and LGPL. The latest
available version is 2.1.1, released on May 1, 2008.

3.3 The datatype package

As the application allows the specification of multiple settings for students or projects it becomes apparent that methods for storing the internal application data are required. This package provides all classes for creating simple data objects. As it remains out of scope for a standalone *Java* application to use a separate database to store and manage its data, a solution of data management with the help of *Java* classes is implemented. Each of the classes represents a special data type with different attributes and methods to alter these values and can be considered as a equivalent of a row in a database's table. Each object must have a unique identifier to be distinguishable from all other objects of the same type. A unique key can either be modelled by defining a variable that serves as primary key and setting it to a different value for each object or determined by looking at the objects 'signature' it is automatically assigned by *Java* when instantiated. *Java* ensures that no two objects can have the same 'signature value', a constraint that cannot be enforced directly in *Java* when a variable is used as identifier. In this case the application logic needs to be written in a way that circumvents the problem of assigning duplicate key values.

Despite its disadvantages, the second approach is still preferable when the object itself is not available to determine its 'signature', but the key variable is known.

Another way to implement data relations is directly linking to the referenced class by defining a variable of the type of the class to be referenced to and then assigning it a data object.

Compared to the flexibility of internal data handling of a database, using data objects has several repercussions on data retrieval speed and flexibility. While databases can directly process queries in standardized languages like SQL that are modelled after natural language and highly flexible in terms of parameters and operators, every non-trivial retrieval query has to be hard-coded when simple data structures as storage for data objects are being used.

Course

The course class is designed as the basic object that stores all the different data objects and takes care of data handling. It also provides methods for complex data retrieval operations.

Objects of the other datatypes Project, Student, Preference, ComplexClass, ProjectComplex and UserComplex are stored in an ArrayList respectively. ArrayList is a convenient structure for storing multiple objects. Like all *Java* collections, it can store a group of objects, known as its elements and has a dynamic size adapting to their number. It implements the List interface. Lists are ordered collections, its elements can either be retrieved by searching or accessed by their integer index.

If elements are to be retrieved from the Collection, all contained elements must be processed. This can be done with the help of an Iterator. To ensure all of the following data object are stored and retrieved in the correct order, each implements the Comparable interface. The method compareTo (Object o) can then be used to establish a sort order between the elements of a collection. JAssign sorts its data objects after the value of its numerical primary key.

Additionally, the course class contains variables for storing the course's number, name and lecturer.

Only one Course object exists for the application at a time, unless the application is reset and a new Course object instantiated.

Preference

An object of this type represents a preference given by a student to a particular project. Each Preference has an attribute of the type Student and one of the type Project. These attributes can be seen as logical pointers to the student and project a preference belongs to. This 'weak entity' concept which depends on the existence of these objects for identification is useful in this case, as a preference detached from its student and project wouldn't make sense. There can only be one preference for every combination of student and project at a time.

The given preference is stored in an integer variable and the boolean value auto denotes whether this preference was assigned by a student or generated automatically during optimization.[1]

Preferences are sorted inside a container by their integer value for Preference. While sorting the preferences is not absolutely necessary and could be neglected, it can increase the readability of the results of a getPrefsByRegnum (String regnum) method call.

Student

Student represents the individual participants of a university course. Based on the assumption that each student has a unique registration number, assigned by the university's administration, this value serves as identifier for objects of this type. It is notable that JAssign allows String values as registration numbers, being more an identifier literal than a number that would be used for mathematical operations. Mainly out of concern that numbers beginning with 0 would be cropped when converted to integer, Strings are permitted. Besides the registration value, each student object contains surname and first name of the person it is representing and values related to optimization, comprising of weight, multiplier value, and a boolean value denoting whether the student should be assigned a project to work on alone. Students are sorted according to the numerical value of their registration number, which makes no additional sorting necessary when the lists or tables displaying all currently available students are being drawn.

Project

Projects are equivalents to the topics or projects that are to be distributed within a university course. Each project receives a numerical ID upon creation, which is derived by the Course class which provides a counter that is incremented each time a project is created. As there is no 'natural' primary key that could be used as identifier for the Project class, a artificial integer key value had to be introduced. Furthermore, each project can have a name, a number and a description. These attributes are not mandatory and thus do

---

[1]See 3.5

not have to fulfill the requirements of identifiers (uniqueness, consistency), instead they can be thought of providing descriptive labels. The ID value is only used internally and remains invisible for the user, while the other attributes remain editable and modifiable. Additionally, a `Project` object contains values related to the optimization process. These are denoting the upper and lower boundaries for the number of participants and multiplier value, respectively. By default, these values are set to 0 which signals the program to determine them automatically. A weight value can be altered to give a program a higher significance. This value is set to 1 by default. [2] Note that the use of project weights is problematic, as it might compromise the actual ranking sequence of a student's preferences.

Categories

The class `ComplexClass` was modelled to store together with `UserComplex` and `ProjectComplex` the information on what is called categories in JAssign. The name `ComplexClass` is a remnant from an early stage of development and conforms to the nomenclature of *OptAssign*. Categories can be regarded as additional constraints that can contain several students or projects whose assignment can be specified in advance. Although empty categories are possible, a useful category can contain 1 to n students (also without any projects, which would render it a primitive type) and 0 to n projects. This relationship is solved by employing the aforementioned classes. Multiple `UserComplex` and `ProjectComplex` objects can be traced back to one `ComplexClass` as the ID used for ComplexClasses is also stored as variable in the two other classes, each of which stands for one student or project assigned to a category.

If the category does not contain any projects, variables can be set to assign the students of the category either all together to one project or distribute them to completely different projects. This information is stored in the `primclass` variable of the `ComplexClass`. Technically speaking, the classes `UserComplex` and `ProjectComplex` resolve the problems arising from a n:m relationship between Students and Categories and Projects and Categories. Both of these classes contain a reference to the `ComplexClass` and its corresponding student/project. This can either be done by storing the identifier

---

[2]Project specific settings can be overwritten by global settings, see 3.6

of both classes in two integer variables or providing the referenced object
directly as a variable.

OptimizePK

OptimizePK stands apart from the other classes of the datatype package. It
serves as a helper class that is used as primary key to retrieve the results
of the optimization from the Hashtable of the Optimized object. This key
consists of the project's and student's identifier.

Figure 3.1 shows the relations between these basic data types in a class
diagram. For the sake of readability it omits methods with obvious function
and little importance to the whole picture.

3.4 The functions package

The *functions* package contains all classes related to importing and exporting or processing the application's data. This includes reading the contents
of a CSV file to be imported (FileImporter), writing the results to a CSV
file (FileExportCSV) or a PDF file (PDFExporter). PDF functionality is
provided by the iText library. Nearly all of the application's events (such as
reactions to button clicks) are defined directly in the main class, to keep
this class reasonably short, the methods for handling the data changes inside the table structures are assembled in a separate file (TableFunctions).
This class provides separate methods for all implemented tables. The corresponding table model is passed as constructor argument, additionally other
arguments can be supplied if required for changing the table data, such as
an Optimized object for tables containing the optimization results.

The package also includes a renderer and an editor extending JTable classes
to draw the results of an optimization using checkboxes and permit changes.

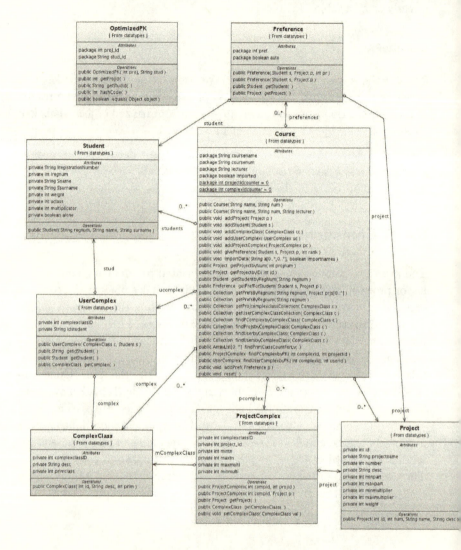

Figure 3.1: The data model used in JAssign

3.5 The optimization package

Everything pertaining to JAssign's optimization is stored in this package. The implementation follows the mathematical model of chapter 5.1. The external library lp_solve is used to build and solve the model. When the 'Optimize' Button in the main application is triggered by the user, the optimization process for the given data is executed. First of all JAssign creates an object for the particular settings the user has specified. This information is stored in an object of the class OptimizeSettings, which is read during the optimization process performed by the Optimize class. Its main method doOptimize takes an object of the type OptimizedSettings as argument. Several auxiliary functions are provided by Optimize. CalculateStandardPrefs() determines the values of missing preferences for each combination of student and project. The value for each non-set preference equals the value of the highest set preference plus one. Although the case that a student is not assigned to one of his lower (better) preferences is unlikely, situations can occur in which no satisfactory solution with the given preferences can be found, especially if the number of preferences is low compared to the number of projects. A Course object contained in the settings is used to perform selection requests that involve iteration through the data containers, which are stored in Course.

As lp_solve works with matrices, the number of variables must be known. This value (labeled NCols) is determined by looking at the number of students, projects and other factors such as soft bounds. Lp_solve then creates the model with the makeLP() method (LP_solve development team, 2008). Once the final model is built and all constraints are set, the objective function is set to minimize, finally the method solve() is called. Lp_solve returns an integer value that indicates if an optimal solution has been attained. If that is not the case, the model is iterated again, until an optimal solution has been reached.

Optimized

If the optimization is successful, a new object of the type Optimized is created. This object stores besides the actual assignments parameters and

---

values that were used during optimization. The constructor calls a method which writes the resulting assignments to a `Hashtable`. A `Hashtable` is a *Java* collection that contains values which are mapped to keys. `OptimizePK`, which consists of the student's and project's identifier, serves as key, while `OptimizedSet` contains the corresponding preference plus a boolean variable denoting if this preference was actually assigned during optimization. One advantage of storing the results in this way is that it is relatively easy to change the assignment of a student by altering the boolean allocation variable.

3.6 The user interface

The GUI designed for interacting with the application consists of one main window which includes a menu bar and 8 tabs for navigation. This section aims at describing the components of the user interface and its user-triggered functionality. Figure 1.1 shows a use-case diagram with typical actions performed by the user. They need not follow a special order and some of them can also be omitted.

The application can be reset anytime by selecting the Program →*reset* menu item. The option Program →exit terminates the program, Help →about shows some basic information on the application.

The Welcome tab (Figure 3.2) is the first tab to be displayed. Information on the course regarding number, name and lecturer can be entered, which is then stored in the `Course` object. A `JToggleButton` allows the user to disable or enable the tooltips. The associated method alters the parameters of the application's global `TooltipManager`.

The Import tab (Figure 3.3) contains all elements related to importing an external CSV file. The entries of a csv-file representing the cells of a table are split with a separation character. The formatting of the CSV data must follow a defined order of elements: **registration number, surname, first name,** P_1, P_2,..., P_n. This character may vary depending on the application used for creating the CSV, so JAssign gives the user the possibility to specify

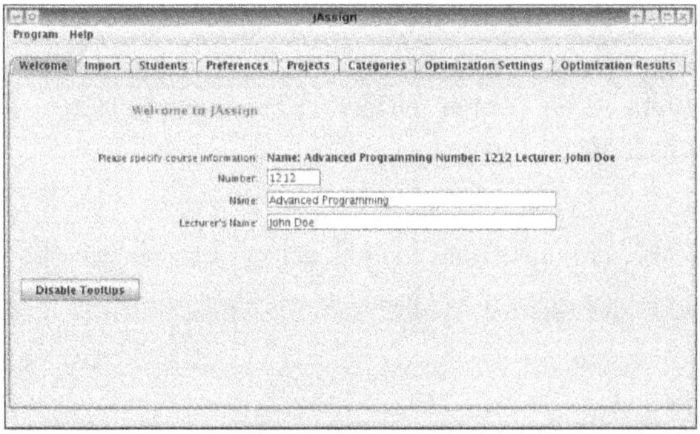

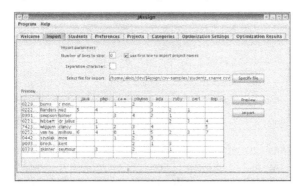

Figure 3.2: Screenshot of JAssign showing the Welcome tab

Figure 3.3: Screenshot of JAssign showing the Import tab

the separation character to be used for importing. By default, this value is the semicolon (;). *Number of lines to skip* allows the user to skip some of the lines of the CSV file. If some of the starting lines of the file should be neglected, this is a useful option. Additionally, the names of the projects can be imported, if desired. The names must be denoted in the first line and follow the formatting of the file. The number of lines to skip need not be adjusted when the project names are imported. *Specify file* pops up a file selection dialog, if a file is selected it is shown in a text field with its complete path. A *Preview* button displays the contents of the file inside a table without importing anything, so the user can make sure s/he selected the right separation character and number of lines to skip. Once a file is selected, pressing the *Import* button will direct `Course` to create objects from the obtained data. `simpleReadInput(...)` reads the contents of a file and returns them as as `Vector` object. The `importData(...)` method of `Course` initializes data objects.

The Students tab (Figure 3.4) displays a list of students, showing registra-

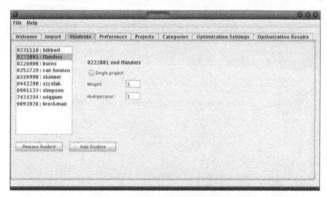

Figure 3.4: Screenshot of JAssign showing the Students tab

tion number and surname. If a student is selected, the parameters related to the optimization are shown. These are *weight* and *multiplier* value. A check box denotes if the currently selected student shall be assigned to be the sole participant of the project s/he is assigned to. The button *Remove Student* deletes the selected entry. *Add Student* opens a popup dialog for the creation of a new student. If a student is added or deleted several update methods are called to redraw all lists and tables affected by the change to synchronize them.

The Preferences tab (Figure 3.5) displays the preferences of the students in an editable table. The first three columns always show the registration number, surname and first name of the student represented in a row, while the remaining columns show the student's preferences. The number of columns is adjusted dynamically to the number of available projects. If project names were imported or created, they are shown in the column headers. A preference can be modified by clicking inside the table and entering a new value.

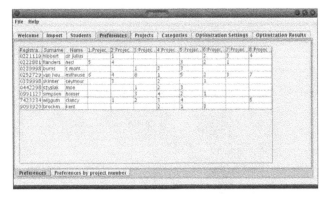

Figure 3.5: Screenshot of JAssign showing the Preferences tab

Likewise the student's name can be changed, but not the registration number. The preferences can be displayed in two ways:

1. Columns ordered by Project id and numerical values of the preferences displayed inside the cells.

2. Columns representing the relative rank of the project from 1 to the amount of projects, while the cells display the project number.

A table listener calls the corresponding method in **TableFunctions** which itself directs the **Course** object to write the changes. If a value is changed, all affected tables and lists are redrawn to enforce consistency.

The Projects tab (Figure 3.6) shows the available projects in a table, where each row represents a project. By default, the entries are sorted by project number. The columns follow the fixed order of **Number, Name, Description, min. participants, max. participants, min. multiplier, max. multiplier** and **weight**. All values can be modified by the user. Listeners call the appropriate function if a change is detected. Two buttons exist to add or remove a project respectively, all lists and tables are redrawn if a change is detected.

The Categories tab (Figure 3.7) allows the definition of additional con-

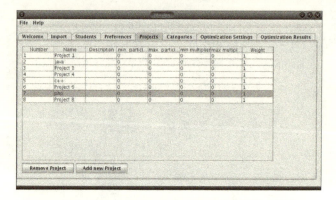

Figure 3.6: Screenshot of JAssign showing the Projects tab

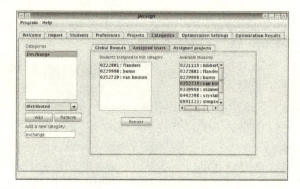

Figure 3.7: Screenshot of JAssign showing the Categories tab

straints. A list shows all available categories, the buttons *Add* and *Remove* modify its content. Before adding the category, a name for it can be set. If an entry of the category list is selected, the entries currently assigned to this category are displayed. A drop down field shows the values available for primitive classes, which can either be *together* (for assigning all students to one project) or *distributed* (if none should work together on one project). When a project is added to the category, these options are no longer available. Another tab container inside the panel allows the user to select if the currently assigned students or projects of the category should be displayed. If desired, global limits for all projects can be set for a category in the

"Global Bounds" tab. If global bounds are set, all projects will be added to the category with the global boundaries. Note that this feature overwrites any existing boundaries for projects previously added to the category. If further adjustment of the boundaries is desired, individual boundaries can be specified for each project in the "assigned projects" tab.

Both "assigned students" and "assigned projects" tab consist of two lists: one displaying the available students or projects while the other list shows the entries currently assigned to the category. By selecting an entry of the first list, it is assigned to the category and displayed inside the second list. Entries can be removed with a *Remove* button. If an assigned project is selected, boundaries can be specified for each entry.

The Optimization Settings tab   (Figure 3.8) Before executing the optimiza-

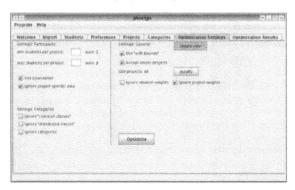

Figure 3.8: Screenshot of JAssign showing the Optimization Settings tab

tion, the user can make some fine-grain adjustments to the optimization settings. The panel that displays these settings offers a simple and an extended view, which shows more of the modifiable optimization parameters. Nearly all parameters are displayed as checkboxes that can either be selected or unselected.

Participants settings:

- *Use boundaries* defines if boundaries are to be used.

- *Ignore project specific data* sets if the project boundaries and settings are read from the data or if the settings specified in this tab are used. (This only applies if "Use boundaries" is selected)

- Two textfields accept values for the upper and lower global boundaries. If no value is entered, JAssign determines appropriate values automatically. An estimation of these values is shown next to the textfield. (This only applies if "Use boundaries" is selected)

General settings:

- *Use "soft Bounds"* selects a soft or strict interpretation of the boundaries. If no solution can be attained, the boundaries can be overwritten in order to make the problem solvable.

- *Accept empty project* ensures that empty projects are permitted which otherwise would cause the optimization to fail because of their boundaries.

- *Ignore student weights* and *Ignore project weights* determines if the respective weights are to be used.

- Projects can be restricted from the optimization. The button *modify* opens a window that allows the user to select the projects to be used.

Category settings:

- "Primitive" categories that enforce a constraint to assign all students of the category to one project can be neglected by selecting *Ignore "common classes"*.

- "Primitive" categories that enforce a constraint to assign all students of the category to different projects can be neglected by selecting *Ignore "distributed classes"*.

- *Ignore categories* directs JAssign to ignore all categories.

The Optimization Results tab   (Figure 3.9) shows the results if the optimization was successful. The results can either be sorted by projects or students, both views use the objects' identifier for sorting, which is displayed in the

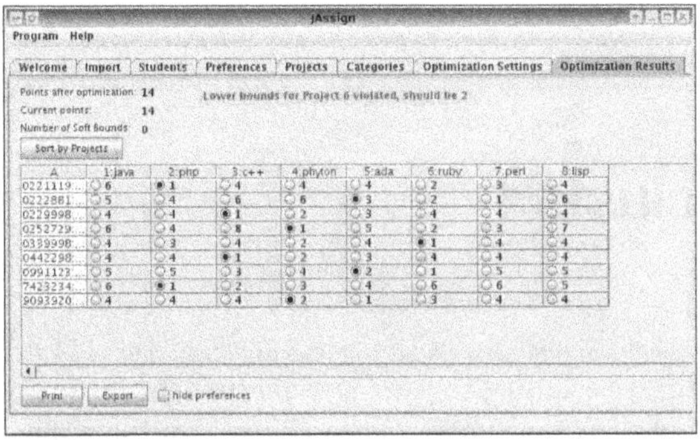

Figure 3.9: Screenshot of JAssign showing the Results tab

rows of the first column. The resulting assignments are shown as radiobuttons, allowing the user to make changes by clicking inside the table and selecting an unselected assignment. The total points of the objective function are displayed, if the user makes alterations by reassigning students, the new sum of the objective functions' points is displayed. The user is warned when the boundaries of a project have been violated. The number of soft bounds that were used to arrive at a solution is also shown.

The results can be exported to PDF using the *Print* button. Depending on the platform the application is running on, the resulting file should open automatically in the PDF viewer that is currently registered with the filetype. *Export* allows the user to create a csv file which can be further processed and formatted in a spreadsheet-application. A checkbox labeled *hide preferences* determines if the preferences that finally were assigned are also written to the file. The formatting of the resulting file depends on the view selected in the results tab.

4 Conclusion

JAssign conveniently automates the assignment of students to topics within university courses according to their preferences used for ranking these topics. The use of *Java* and its *Swing* toolkit makes the application and its graphical user interface basically platform-independent. The application's graphical user interface facilitates interaction with the program to a great extend and allows the user to import, export and modify the data and specify constraints for the optimization process. The external libraries `lp_solve` and *iText* are used to solve the linear optimization problem and export the results to PDF respectively. JAssign is based on the functionality of a previous, web-based application (*OptAssign*), from which it inherits portions of the optimization process.

JAssign will run on any machine with a *Java Runtime Environment* and the libraries of `lp_solve` installed.

5 Appendix

5.1 The optimization model used

In the field of mathematics, linear programming deals with the optimization of a linear objective function over a set constricted by linear equality and inequality constraints. On diverse fields of application, linear programming can be used to solve generally every problem where an optimal distribution of limited resources on competing activities is desired. "Linear and integer programming have proved valuable for modeling many and diverse types of problems in planning, routing, scheduling, assignment, and design" (M. Berkelaar and Notebaert, 2008).
The model presented here for the specific problem of assigning students to a limited number of courses with regard to their individual preferences is based on Meyer (2008) and the extensions used for the *OptAssign* application in Waglechner (2008). The optimization model of *OptAssign* serves as a starting point for JAssign's optimization and is taken with only minor modifications. Apart from the introduction of project weights the model of *OptAssign* is closely followed. Therefore only a basic description of the underlying model will be given here, including the mathematical formulations. The complete mathematical model with all extensions is provided at the end of the appendix.

Basic concepts

As mentioned before, the optimization process aims at assigning students (S) to available projects (T), taking into account the students' preferences and limitations of group size. Each student is allowed to rank these projects by assigning them whole numbers. $P_{at} \in N, s \in S, t \in T$. Project t is

---

given preference over t' if $P_{st} < P_{st'}$. Assignments are represented by binary variables $A_{st} \in \{0, 1\}$. Neglecting further constraints, the optimal solution would be assigning each student to the project s/he prefers most. As a consequence, a lower sum of the preferences results in higher overall satisfaction. One constraint is the limitation that each student can only be assigned to one project. For each project, different upper U_t and lower L_t boundaries can exist.

$$\sum_{s,t} P_{st}A_{st} \to \text{min!} \qquad (5.1)$$

s.t.

(Atomicity) $\qquad \sum_{t} A_{st} = 1 \qquad \forall s \in S \qquad (5.2)$

(Lower bounds) $\qquad \sum_{s} A_{st} \geq L_t \qquad \forall t \in T \qquad (5.3)$

(Upper bounds) $\qquad \sum_{s} A_{st} \leq U_t \qquad \forall t \in T \qquad (5.4)$

(Binarity) $\qquad A_{st} \in \{0, 1\} \qquad \forall s \in S, t \in T \qquad (5.5)$

(Preferences) $\qquad P_{st} \in \mathbb{N} \qquad \forall s \in S, t \in T \qquad (5.6)$

(Bounds) $\qquad L_t \in \mathbb{N}_0, \ U_t \in \mathbb{N}, \ L_t \leq U_t \qquad \forall t \in T \qquad (5.7)$

Weights and multipliers

Additionally, weights and multipliers are introduced into the model. Students or projects can be deliberately preferred by customly assigning weights $W_s^S \in \mathbb{R}^+$, $W_t^T \in \mathbb{R}^+$.

$$\sum_{s,t} \mathbf{W_s^S} \mathbf{W_t^T} P_{st}A_{st} \to \text{min!}$$

(Weights) $\qquad \mathbf{W_s^S} \in \mathbb{R}^+, \mathbf{W_t^T} \in \mathbb{R}^+ \quad \forall s \in S, t \in T \qquad (5.8)$

A student can be favored by assigning him a weight greater than 1. All preferences in the target function are then multiplied by this weight which increases the difference between the specified preferences by W_a. This leads to an increase of the target function by $W_s > 1$ if the student is assigned a project with a higher preference value. Additionally, weights for the projects W_t are introducted which are multiplied by the students' weights. A project with a higher weight is then preferred over others. This feature should be used with caution, as it might involuntarily distort the students' individual rankings.

Furthermore it can be desired to give some students a higher workload, which can be done by assigning them multipliers.
If a student has a multiplier greater than 1, s/he will occupy more than one place and the project's boundaries will be saturated more quickly, thus the project will have fewer participants. Multipliers M_s therefore affect the upper and lower group boundaries.

$$\text{(Lower bounds)} \qquad \sum_s \mathbf{M_s} A_{st} \geq L_t \qquad \forall t \in T \qquad (5.9)$$

$$\text{(Upper bounds)} \qquad \sum_s \mathbf{M_s} A_{st} \leq U_t \qquad \forall t \in T \qquad (5.10)$$

$$\textbf{(Multipliers)} \qquad M_s \in \mathbb{N} \qquad \forall s \in S \qquad (5.11)$$

Extensions

Categories

The optimization model also allows the specification of categories, which are prespecified conditions for the assignment of students. Put into different words it allows defining sub-groups with several students and special parameters. A category can contain several students which are treated according to special attributes that can be specified in advance. 3 types of categories are available:

1. All students of the category can be distributed to different projects.

2. All students of the category can be allocated to the same project.

3. Several projects can be assigned to one category. (Additionally, all projects can be taken into a category with global boundaries.)

The first two variants are also referred to as the primitive type in the *OptAssign* documentation.

To increase the granularity of the categories and allow the specification of additional constraints, one or several projects can be assigned to each category. Further options can be specified for each project (note that they solely exist within the category and are independent from the values directly specified for the project). This includes setting boundaries for these projects. This variant is referred to as the complex type in the *OptAssign* documentation.

Empty projects

Though it can be conjectured that a course lecturer wants to distribute all available projects, a situation might arise in which the number of available topics exceeds the demand. When Projects are left without participants, no optimal solution can be attained as the sum of the lower boundaries for the number of participants would be violated. To ensure the solvability of the problem another constraint needs to be introduced into the model that allows the program to stray from the lower bounds of a group, in a way that either the lower bounds of a project are active or the 'empty project' constraint applies.

Individual projects

Until now the formation of groups for each project was assumed. It might be desired by the lecturer to let certain students work alone on an individual project, for example if the student has to write a bachelor thesis. Evidently the model needs to be extended by another constraint to allow individual projects.

Soft Bounds

Given all the previously defined constraints, the overall solvability of individual optimization problems might be poor if all the restrictions have to be met exactly. In case the boundaries are too narrow to encompass every student and several unassigned students remain, the optimization will fail. To improve the solvability of these problems caused by 'excess' students a relaxation of the boundaries is introduced that applies in case the problem would be unsolvable otherwise.

The mathematical model used

Combining all modifications, the final model becomes:

$$\sum_{s,t} W_s^s W_t^t P_{st} A_{st} + B \sum_t (E_t + \sum_k E_{kt}^c) \rightarrow \text{min!} \tag{5.12}$$

s.t.

Constraints :

(Atomicity) $\qquad\qquad\qquad \sum_t A_{st} = 1 \qquad \forall s \in S \qquad$ (5.13)

(Lower bounds) $\qquad\qquad \sum_s A_{st} + B \cdot D_t^g \geq L_t \qquad \forall t \in T \qquad$ (5.14)

(Upper bounds) $\qquad\qquad \sum_s A_{st} - B \cdot D_t^g \leq U_t \qquad \forall t \in T \qquad$ (5.15)

(Lower subbounds) $\qquad \sum_s C_{kst} M_s A_{st} + B \cdot D_t^g \geq L_{kt}^c \qquad \forall k \in K, t \in T \qquad$ (5.16)

(Upper subbounds) $\qquad \sum_s C_{kst} M_s A_{st} - B \cdot D_t^g - E_{kt}^c \leq U_{kt}^c \qquad \forall k \in K, t \in T, s \in S$

$$\tag{5.17}$$

(Individual projects) $\qquad \sum_s (1 - G_s) A_{st} + D_t^i = 1 \qquad \forall t \in T \qquad$ (5.18)

$$\sum_s G_s A_{st} - B \cdot D_t^i \leq 0 \qquad \forall t \in T \qquad \text{(5.19)}$$

(Empty projects) $\qquad\qquad \sum_s A_{st} - B \cdot D_t^e \leq 0 \qquad \forall t \in T \qquad$ (5.20)

(XOR conditions) $\qquad\qquad D_t^g + D_t^i + D_t^e = 2 \qquad \forall t \in T \qquad$ (5.21)

Variables :

(Topic assignments) $\qquad\qquad\qquad A_{st} \in \{0, 1\} \quad \forall s \in S, t \in T$ (5.22)

(Excess students) $\qquad\qquad\qquad E_t, E_{kt}^c \in \{0, 1\} \quad \forall k \in K, t \in T$ (5.23)

(Switching variables) $\qquad D_t^g, D_t^i, D_t^e, Z^{tog}, Z^{dis} \in \{0, 1\} \quad \forall t \in T$ (5.24)

Parameters :

(Preferences) $\qquad\qquad\qquad\qquad P_{st} \in \mathbb{N} \quad \forall s \in S, t \in T$ (5.25)

(Weights) $\qquad\qquad\qquad W_s^S, W_t^T \in \mathbb{R}^+ \quad \forall s \in S, t \in T$ (5.26)

(Multipliers) $\qquad\qquad\qquad\qquad M_s \in \mathbb{N} \quad \forall s \in S$ (5.27)

(Bounds) $\qquad L_t \in \mathbb{N}_0, U_t \in \mathbb{N}, L_t \leq U_t \quad \forall t \in T$ (5.28)

(Subbounds) $\qquad\qquad\qquad L_{kt}^c, U_{kt}^c \in \mathbb{N}_0 \quad \forall k \in K, t \in T$ (5.29)

(Group projects) $\qquad\qquad\qquad\qquad G_s \in \{0, 1\} \quad \forall s \in S$ (5.30)

(Categories) $\qquad\qquad\qquad\qquad C_{ks} \in \{0, 1\} \quad \forall k \in K, s \in S$ (5.31)

Bibliography

Lawler, E. and Wood, D. (1966). Branch-and-bound methods: A survey.

Lowagie, B. (2008). *iText Documentation FAQ, Available from:* *http://itext.ugent.be/library/faq.php.*

LP_solve development team (2008). *Lp_solve API, Available from:* *http://lpsolve.sourceforge.net/5.1/lp_solveAPIreference.htm*

M. Berkelaar, K. E. and Notebaert, P. (2008). *Lpsolve reference guide, version 5.5.0.12, Available from: http://lpsolve.sourceforge.net*

Meyer, D. (2008). *OptAssign - A Web-based Decision Support System, Mathematical model.*

O'Conner, J. (2007). *Using the Swing Application Framework (JSR 296), Available from: http://java.sun.com/developer/technicalArticles/javase/swingappfr/.*

Sun Microsystems (2006). *Java Specification Request 296: Swing Application Framework, Available from: http://jcp.org/en/jsr/detail?id=296*

Sun Microsystems (2008a). *Creating a GUI with JFC/Swing, Available from: http://java.sun.com/docs/books/tutorial/uiswing/.*

Sun Microsystems (2008b). *Java GUI Application Learning Trail, Available from: http://www.netbeans.org/kb/trails/matisse.html*

Sun Microsystems (2008c). *Java Platform, Standard Edition 6, API Specification, Available from: http://java.sun.com/javase/6/docs/api/.*

Sun Microsystems (2008d). *Netbeans Help.*

Waglechner, C. (2008). *OptAssign - Implementierung einer Web-Applikation zur optimalen Zuordnung von Studenten zu Projekten auf Basis von Java-EE.*